CE Web Services

simplifying HTML

By James P. Collier II

CE Web Services

Simplifying HTML

ISBN-10: 1477559655
ISBN-13: 978-1477559659

For my boys - - who might be interested someday.

Table of Contents

Preface

It's not often that books and resources get right to the point with practical examples and information. The best resources, I have found, are generally online. There is a wealth of knowledge available for those who take the time to find it and some of the best examples exist in live sites where designers and developers have implemented HTML and CSS in creative ways.

I have prepared this collection for my sons who have recently expressed an interest in web development. One son is very bright and self sufficient, while my other son (who is also bright and the most interested and persistent) has autism and experiences challenges with comprehension. It's my hope that a clearly prepared text describing the use of HTML will help him understand and learn that in which he appears to be interested.

I'm not planning on spending time discussing the history of the web and web development; rather I want to focus on the practical use of HTML.

Just for the record, I'm in no way an expert or authority on all things web. I'm just a sideline developer with a completely different day job who happens to enjoy creating websites for those less inclined.

Conventions Used in This Book

Typographic and layout styles are used to separate examples from instruction. The following icons are used throughout this text to describe the type of code block being presented.

 Example

 Exercise

 Warning

 Correct Method

 Incorrect Method

Code samples are provided in the following format:

```
#container {
   position: absolute;
   right: 0;
   top: 0;
}
```

With updates to code samples indicated in bold text:

```
#container {
   position: absolute;
   right: 0;
   top: 0;
   width: 200px;
   text-align: left;
}
```

Getting the Bug

Cultivating an interest in web development is the first step to doing great things online. We've all been there, surfing the web, and all of a sudden the most inspiring site hits you in the face. Wow! What a moment. That's the moment you decide to learn how to create something that might affect someone else is the same manner. That's when you decide to learn how to build or write content for the web. Now the journey begins and you take that first step. This little guide is intended to help with the basics and serve as a handy reference at any point down the road.

For the Record

HTML, the primary language of the web which defines the basic structure of any page viewed in a web browser, stands for:

Hyper Text Markup Language

CSS, the means of defining style elements outside of the HTML (that is to say, separate from the content), stands for:

Cascading Style Sheet

Chapter 1

Tools of the Trade

Tools of the Trade

Truth be told, developing in HTML and CSS does not require costly software. If you have a computer, you already have the tools you need; on a Windows computer you can use Notepad while on a Mac you can use TextEdit. These applications do not offer any special features, just a simple white page for you to work on.

Here are a few applications (some free and some not) that try to improve on these basic applications with varying degrees of sophistication. You will likely want to try out a few to decide what works best for you.

Windows HTML / CSS / FTP Applications

As you might expect there are more HTML editors for Windows then there are for Mac. Here is a list of both free and paid applications, all of which I have used at one time or another.

Free Applications

- Bluefish
  http://bluefish.openoffice.nl/
- Crimson Editor
  http://www.crimsoneditor.com/
- EditRocket
  http://www.editrocket.com/features/html_editor.html
- FileZilla
  http://filezilla-project.org/
- First Page 2006
  http://www.evrsoft.com/1stpage3.shtml
- NoteTab Lite
  http://www.fookes.com/
- PSPad
  http://www.pspad.com/
- TopStyle Lite
  http://topstyle.en.softonic.com/

Paid Applications

- Adobe DreamWeaver
  http://www.adobe.com/products/dreamweaver.html
- TopStyle 4
  http://www.topstyle4.com/

Mac HTML / CSS / FTP Applications

Until a year ago I was a pretty committed windows user and did not bother too much about Mac applications. Now that I have a Mac, I have a completely new appreciation for what I have been missing. I am still getting used to things, but working on a Mac is an enjoyable experience.

Free Applications

- Bluefish
  http://bluefish.openoffice.nl/
- Aptana Studio
  http://www.aptana.com/
- EditRocket
  http://www.editrocket.com/features/html_editor.html
- FileZilla
  http://filezilla-project.org/
- TextWrangler
  http://www.barebones.com/products/textwrangler/

Paid Applications

- Adobe Dreamweaver
  http://www.adobe.com/products/dreamweaver.html
- BBEdit
  http://www.barebones.com/products/bbedit/
- Coda
  http://www.panic.com/coda/
- Espresso
  http://macrabbit.com/espresso/

Chances are pretty good that I have missed a number of good ones, but you can search the web for more candidates that may work out better for you.

Lorem Ipsum

Lorem ipsum is a great way to fill a page with textual content in order to demonstrate the visual representation of a web page without being consumed with the content on the page. It's a great way to look at your page design to determine how your graphics and stylistic layout will look. Despite the occasional challenge with people who focus more on the text, I use lorem ipsum all the time when preparing a design for a client.

Here is how Lorem ipsum is described on Wikipedia:

> “ In publishing and graphic design, lorem ipsum[p][1] is placeholder text (filler text) commonly used to demonstrate the graphics elements of a document or visual presentation, such as font, typography, and layout.
>
> http://en.wikipedia.org/wiki/Lorem_ipsum

To help you create this filler text, there are websites and applications designed to generate lorem ipsum. Here are a few that I use regularly:

- Lorem Ipsum (web app)
  http://www.lipsum.com/
- LittleIpsum (Mac)
  http://littleipsum.com/

The following image is an example of a web page using lorum ipsum filler text.

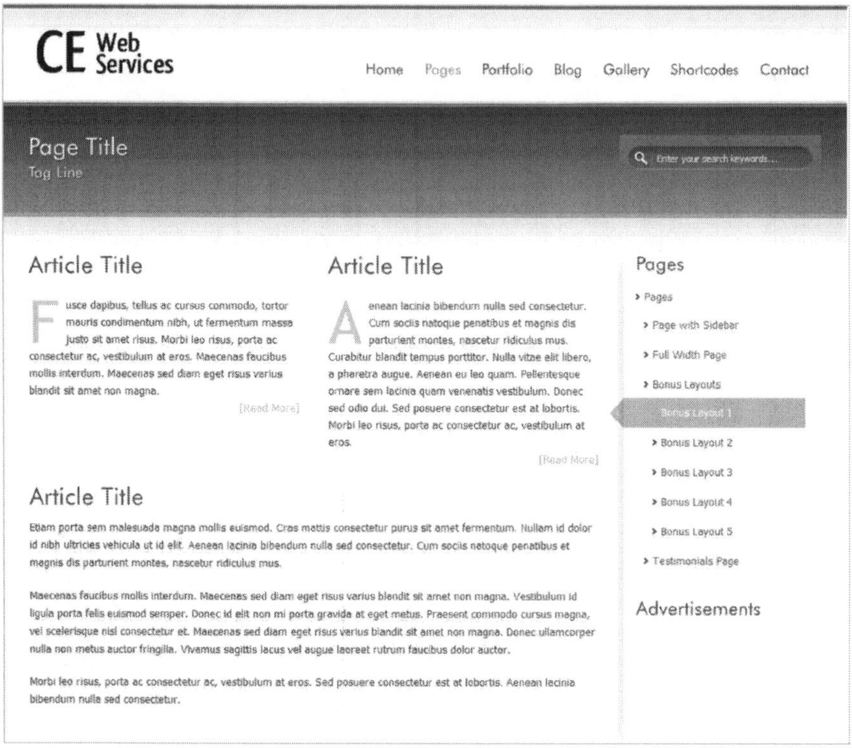

You can see how lorem ipsum fills the page as if real content were actually on the page.

Folders and File Names

HTML (Hypertext Markup Language)

HTML documents are saved with either the .htm or .html file extension. There really is no difference between the two, so the choice of which file extension to use is up to you. But once you have made your choice, I recommend you stick to the same extension for all the pages in one site.

Here is an example of the same file with both extensions:

```
index.htm
index.html
```

CSS (Cascading Style Sheets)

CSS documents are saved with the .css file extension. Here is an example a file using the CSS file extension.

```
style.css
```

Folder Structure

When developing a web page in HTML, it is a best practice to keep all related files in the same folder or in sub-folders to the parent.

Your files may look like this (all in one folder).

```
Web Site [root folder]
   - footer.png
   - header.png
   - index.html
   - style.css
```

Or like this (separating different types of files into sub-folders).

```
Web Site [root folder]
   css [folder]
      - style.css
   images [folder]
      - footer.png
      - header.png
   - index.html
```

I would like to emphasize two important points here:

1. Web addresses are case sensitive, which include your directories, subdirectories, and individual filenames.
2. Spaces in folders and filenames should not be used. Rather you should use either an underscore(_), a dash(-), or Camel Case notation (see the section on "Spaces" on page 13).

Absolute and Relative URLs

To access a file on the web, a web address, or URL, for the file must be entered into the address field of a web browser. URL stands for "Uniform Resource Locator." A URL is the address of a specific Web site or file on the Internet. Here is an example of a URL:

```
http://www.cewebservices.com/studio/index.html
----- -------------------- ------ ---------
  1             2                3       4
```

1. **Protocol** - The type of resource it is addressing. The most common protocol is HyperText Transfer Protocol (HTTP).
2. **Domain** - The host name of the computer from which the file can be located.
3. **Folder/Directory** - Any folder or sub-folder that further defines the location of the HTML page or related resource below the domain.
4. **Filename** - The specific file being addressed. This can be any web file in the domain or specified folder.

A URL describing the location of a file on the web which includes the protocol, a domain, a folder (if necessary), and a specific filename is an “absolute” URL.

A URL which includes only a folder (if necessary) and a specific filename is a “relative” domain. A relative domain uses the protocol and domain of the current page URL and then appends the relative domain to form the complete URL.

Case Sensitivity

Web addresses are case sensitive, which include your directories, subdirectories, and individual filenames.

In this example, "studio" and "STUDIO" are not the same. They do not technically point to the same location.

http://www.cewebservices.com/**studio**/index.html

http://www.cewebservices.com/**STUDIO**/index.html

Be sure to consider the case of the characters used in folders and file names and be consistent in the case you decide to use. See the next section "Spaces" for some examples of folder and filenames.

Spaces

Spaces in folder names and filenames should not be used. Instead you should use either an underscore(_), a dash(-), or Camel Case notation.

Here is an incorrect example of using a space in a folder name:

```
photo gallery
```

Here are some correct examples of how you might adjust your folder names in preparation for use on the web:

Underscore

```
photo_gallery
```

Dash

```
photo-gallery
```

camelCase

With camel case, the first letter of the entity is lowercase and the first letter of each subsequent concatenated word is capitalized.

```
photoGallery
```

Wikipedia describes camel Case as follows:

> Camel case is the practice of writing compound words or phrases in which the elements are joined without spaces, with each element's initial letter capitalized.
>
> http://en.wikipedia.org/wiki/CamelCase

Here is an incorrect example of using a space in a filename:

```
summer fun.png
```

Here are some correct examples of how you might adjust your filenames in preparation for use on the web:

Underscore

```
summer_fun.png
```

Dash

```
summer-fun.png
```

camelCase

```
summerFun.png
```

What's a web browser?

Let us take a look at how a web browser is defined on Wikipedia:

> A web browser is a software application for retrieving, presenting, and traversing information resources on the World Wide Web. ... A web browser can also be defined as an application, software, or program designed to enable users to access, retrieve and view documents and other resources on the Internet.
>
> http://en.wikipedia.org/wiki/Web_browser

It is with a web browser that you are able to view the HTML pages and content you are creating. Here are the heavy hitters in the browser world:

Chrome (by Google)

http://www.google.com/chrome/

Firefox (by Mozilla)

http://www.mozilla.com/firefox/fx/

Internet Explorer (by Mocrosoft)

http://windows.microsoft.com/en-US/internet-explorer/products/ie/home

Opera (by Opera Software)

http://www.opera.com/

Safari (by Apple)

http://www.apple.com/safari/

Browser Testing

Since the beginning of the web, browser manufacturers have been at odds regarding the proper rendering of HTML elements. As a result, an HTML page viewed in one browser may not appear exactly the same in another. Fortunately, with each passing version the standards by which browser manufacturers render HTML are becoming increasingly similar. Unfortunately, with each passing version the end users who are viewing HTML pages are doing so on an increasing number of browser versions. This means that web developers face a growing number of browsers and browser versions in which to test.

So what can you do? You can either install and test with as many browsers and browser versions as you are able to lay your hands on – yuk! – or you can use some online tools to help you compare your HTML pages in different rendering engines. Here are a few testing tools that might help you in this effort:

- Free
    - Browser Shots
      http://browsershots.org/
    - Expression Web SuperPreview
      http://expression.microsoft.com/en-us/dd565874.aspx
    - Gomez Cross Browser Test
      http://www.gomez.com/google-adwords/cross-browser-compatibility-test/
- Paid
    - Adobe Browser Lab
      https://browserlab.adobe.com/en-us/index.html
    - Cross Browser Testing
      http://crossbrowsertesting.com
    - Scout
      http://saucelabs.com/docs/scout/

Chapter 2

HTML 4 Elements

HTML 4 Elements

HTML 5, the newest proposed update to HTML is a specification that improves on many of the capabilities of HTML 4. These improvements make elements that previously required JavaScript and other non-HTML objects to make the presentation of HTML pages more dynamic an inherent part of HTML. Unfortunately, the final specification and adoption of HTML 5 will continue to be debated for some time as browser manufacturers make updates in their rendering engine that nudge us closer to the proposed specification for HTML 5.

Even with the update to an enhanced HTML 5 specification, most of the core components of the current HTML 4 will continue to be meaningful in purpose and practice. That said you can not wholesale remove the need to know how to use the still relevant HTML 4 elements even as we look to the future of the language specification.

This chapter will describe the use of HTML 4 elements with examples using proper syntax. The elements described here are organized into like classifications to hopefully make it easy to see how some elements relate to one other.

Basic Page Structure

Doctype aside, there are three main sections of a HTML page.

- The `<html> ... </html>` tag describes the parent container for everything on the HTML page. Except for the doctype, everything on the HTML page resides inside these tags.
- The `<head> ... </head>` tag contains information about the HTML page and provide links to other files (like cascading style sheets and JavaScript files) which are included as a part of the browser rendered page without actually being embedded In the HTML page itself. None of the elements contained in this section are visible on the page itself.
- The `<body> ... </body>` tag contains all of the visual elements of the HTML page. Depending on the styling of the page, everything within the body tags is what you see on the page.

Here is an example of the basic HTML page structure:

```
<!DOCTYPE HTML>

<html lang="en”>

<head>

   <title>Page Title</title>

</head>

<body>

<h1>Page Header</>
<p>This is a paragraph</p>

</body>

</html>
```

Doctype

One of the most significant changes in the HTML 5 specification is the consolidation of the many complicated doctypes into a single reference. Here are examples of HTML 4 doctypes that told a web browser which version of the markup language a given page was written.

HTML 4.01 Strict

```
<!DOCTYPE HTML PUBLIC "-//W3C//DTD HTML 4.01//EN"
"http://www.w3.org/TR/html4/strict.dtd">
```

HTML 4.01 Transitional

```
<!DOCTYPE HTML PUBLIC "-//W3C//DTD HTML 4.01
Transitional//EN"
"http://www.w3.org/TR/html4/loose.dtd">
```

HTML 4.01 Frameset

```
<!DOCTYPE HTML PUBLIC "-//W3C//DTD HTML 4.01
Frameset//EN"
"http://www.w3.org/TR/html4/frameset.dtd">
```

XHTML 1.0 Strict

```
<!DOCTYPE html PUBLIC "-//W3C//DTD XHTML 1.0
Strict//EN" "http://www.w3.org/TR/xhtml1/DTD/xhtml1-
strict.dtd">
```

XHTML 1.0 Transitional

```
<!DOCTYPE html PUBLIC "-//W3C//DTD XHTML 1.0
Transitional//EN"
"http://www.w3.org/TR/xhtml1/DTD/xhtml1-
transitional.dtd">
```

XHTML 1.0 Frameset

```
<!DOCTYPE html PUBLIC "-//W3C//DTD XHTML 1.0
Frameset//EN" "http://www.w3.org/TR/xhtml1/DTD/xhtml1-
frameset.dtd">
```

XHTML 1.1

```
<!DOCTYPE html PUBLIC "-//W3C//DTD XHTML 1.1//EN"
"http://www.w3.org/TR/xhtml11/DTD/xhtml11.dtd">
```

You can see how one might be somewhat confused between the various HTML 4 doctypes. Luckily HTML 5 has fixed this problem and makes the doctype reference in one simple declaration.

In HTML 5, the doctype simply looks like this:

```
<!DOCTYPE HTML>
```

Talk about a breath of fresh air. No more headaches over the proper doctype declaration. So, to keep things forward thinking, all of the code examples in this text will use the HTML 5 doctype declaration.

Top Level Elements

Top level elements include:

- <html>
- <head>
- <body>

<html>

The <html> is a required element on every HTML page.

Syntax `<html> ... </html>`

Standard

Attribute	Value
lang	en

```
<!DOCTYPE HTML>

<html lang="en">
<head>

...

</head>
<body>

...

</body>
</html>
```

Note: For other ISO 639-1 language codes, visit the following Library of Congress language standards page:

http://www.loc.gov/standards/iso639-2/php/code_list.php

<head>

The <head> is a required element on every HTML page and contains header information about the document.

Syntax `<head> ... </head>`

```
<!DOCTYPE HTML>

<html lang="en”>

<head>

...

</head>

<body>

...

</body>

</html>
```

<body>

The <body> is a required element on every HTML page.

Syntax `<body> ... </body>`

Standard

Attribute	Value
class	classname
id	unique id
style	inline style

```
<!DOCTYPE HTML>
<html lang="en”>
<head>
...
</head>
<body>
...
</body>
</html>
```

Head Elements

Head elements are those elements that reside inside the `<head> ... </head>` tag. In this section we will cover the following HTML elements:

- <base>
- <link>
- <meta>
- <script>
- <style>
- <title>

<base>

The `<base>` element defines the global base location and target behavior of links on the HTML page.

Syntax `<base>`

Standard

Attribute	Value
href base "absolute" URL for all relative links	URL
target	_blank _parent _self _top

The following example demonstrates the use of the <base> tag to specify the base "absolute" URL for all relative links on the page.

```
<head>

<base href="http://www.google.com/" />

</head>

<body>

<img src="images/smiley.gif" />

</body>
```

In this example, the relative image location is combined with the absolute base URL to point to the image. The result is:

http://www.google.com/images/smiley.gif

The following example demonstrates the use of the <base> tag to specify the behavior of links on the page.

```
<head>

<base target="_blank" />

</head>

<body>

<a href="http://www.google.com">Google</a>

</body>
```

In this example, the Google link (as well as any other links added to the page) will open in a new browser window.

The global base location and target behavior specified in the <head> of the page can be overridden with inline absolute URLs and inline target behaviors.

<link>

The <link> element defines the relationship between documents.

Syntax `<link>`

Optional

Attribute	Value
href absolute or relative location of the linked document	URL
media media appropriate for link	screen print all
rel relationship to link	stylesheet
type content-type of link	text/html text/css text/javascript

```
<head>

<link href="style.css" rel="stylesheet"
type="text/css" media="screen">

</head>
```

Embedding an external style sheet not only applies the styles to the linked HTML page, but allows the same styles to be linked to other HTML pages as well. This method of linking style documents to multiple HTML pages creates a cascading effect. So when a style change is made to the external style sheet, the effecting change is reflected in all HTML pages to which the updated style sheet is linked.

<meta>

The `<meta>` element provides metadata about the HTML page.

Syntax `<meta>`

Required

Attribute	Value
content content of the meta information	text

Optional

Attribute	Value
http-equiv	content-type
name property name	author description keywords generator revised

```
<head>

<meta http-equiv="content-type"
content="text/html;charset=UTF-8" />

<meta name="description" content="A description of the
HTML 4 meta tag." />

<meta name="keywords"
content="HTML,CSS,XML,JavaScript" />

<meta name="author" content="James Collier" />

</head>
```

<script>

The `<script>` element includes client side script in the HTML page.

Syntax `<script> ... </script>`

Required

Attribute	Value
type content-type of scripting language	text/html text/css text/javascript

Optional

Attribute	Value
charset encoding of external script	ISO-8859-1
src external script location	URL

```
<head>

<script type="text/javascript" src="file.js"
charset="ISO-8859-1"></script>

</head>
```

This example demonstrates linking an external JavaScript file to the HTML page, thus making the functions in the JavaScript file available to the page.

<style>

The <style> element embeds style information in the HTLM page. You can embed as many style elements in the head as may be necessary.

Syntax `<style> ... </style>`

Required

Attribute	Value
type	text/css

Optional

Attribute	Value
media	screen print all

The following example shows embedding style information directly in the HTML page. This type of style embedding is only relevant to the page on which it resides; it has no impact on other HTML pages.

```
<head>

<style type="text/css" media=screen>
<!--
  body   { background: #000; color: #666; }
  p      { margin: 10px 5px; }
  .block { border: 1px solid #000000; }
-->
</style>

</head>
```

<title>

The <title> element is used to describe the HTML page. The title is visible to the page visitor in the title bar of the browser window.

Syntax `<title> ... </title>`

```
<head>

<title>Page Title</title>

</head>
```

Basic Page Structure with Header Elements

Here is a browser preview of an HTML page utilizing the <head> elements described in this section.

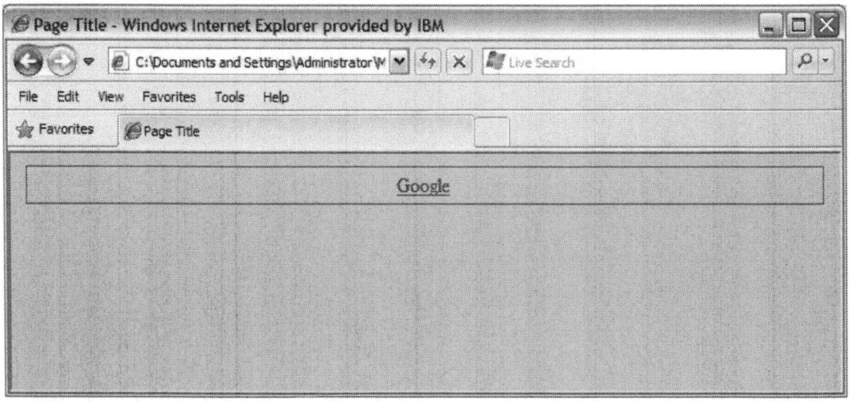

The following is the HTML code which produced the previous browser example.

```
<!DOCTYPE HTML>

<html lang="en">

<head>

<title>Page Title</title>

<meta http-equiv="content-type" content="text/html;charset=UTF-8" />
<meta name="description" content="A description of the HTML 4 meta tag." />
<meta name="keywords" content="HTML,CSS,XML,JavaScript" />
<meta name="author" content="James Collier" />

<base target="_blank" />

<style type="text/css">
body
{
    background: #BFCFFF;
    color: #666666;
}

p
{
    margin: 10px 5px;
}

.block
{
    border: 1px solid #4070FF;
    padding: 5px;
    text-align: center;
}
</style>

</head>

<body>

<p class="block"><a href="http://www.google.com">Google</a></p>

</body>
```

Block Level Elements

Block level elements reside within the `<body> ... </body>` of the HTML page and define specific block elements. In this section we will cover the following HTML elements:

- <blockquote>
- <div>
- Headers <h1> – <h6>
- <p>
-
- <hr />
- <pre>

Most HTML elements require a matching, or closing, tag in order to be formed correctly. For instance, the <h1> tag is properly closed with a </h1> matching closing tag.

```
<body>

<h1>Heading Level 1</h1>

</body>
```

In instances where an HTML element does not require a separate closing tag as with the horizontal rule, the element should be closed using a single forward slash before closing the element.

```
<body>

<hr />

</body>
```

<blockquote>

The `<blockquote>` element defines a block used to identify a long quotation from an external source.

Syntax `<blockquote> ... </blockquote>`

Optional

Attribute	Value
cite source of a quotation	URL

Standard

Attribute	Value
class	classname
id	unique identifier
style	style definition
title	extra element information

```
<body>

<blockquote class="quote" id="definition1"
style="border: 1px solid #E0DFE3; padding: 3px;"
cite="http://en.wikipedia.org/">

The blockquote element is used to indicate the
quotation of a large section of text from another
source.

</blockquote>

</body>
```

<div>

The `<div>` element defines a generic block-level container.

Syntax `<div> ... </div>`

Optional

Attribute	Value
align	left right center justify

Standard

Attribute	Value
class	classname
id	unique identifier
style	style definition
title	extra element information

```
<body>

<div style="background-color:#CCCCCC; border: 1px
dashed #0033FF; padding: 3px;">
This is a &lt;div&gt; block level element.
</div>

</body>
```

Headers (<h1> – <h6>)

The h1 – h6 elements define heading levels 1 – 6. Generally, there should only be one h1 element to mark the most important heading for the page.

Syntax

```
<h1> ... </h1>
<h2> ... </h2>
<h3> ... </h3>
<h4> ... </h4>
<h5> ... </h5>
<h6> ... </h6>
```

Standard

Attribute	Value
class	classname
id	unique identifier
style	style definition
title	extra element information

```
<body>
<h1>Heading Level 1</h1>
<h2>Heading Level 2</h2>
<h3>Heading Level 3</h3>
<h4>Heading Level 4</h4>
<h5>Heading Level 5</h5>
<h6>Heading Level 6</h6>
</body>
```

<p>

The <p> element defines a paragraph.

Syntax `<p> ... </p>`

Standard

Attribute	Value
class	classname
id	unique identifier
style	style definition
title	extra element information

```
<body>
<p>The quick brown fox jumped over the lazy dog.</p>
</body>
```


The `<br />` element inserts a single line break (or soft return).

Syntax `<br />`

Standard

Attribute	Value
class	classname
id	unique identifier
style	style definition
title	extra element information

```
<body>

<br />

</body>
```

<hr />

The `<hr />` element defines a horizontal rule within a block.

Syntax `<hr />`

Standard

Attribute	Value
class	classname
id	unique identifier
style	style definition
title	extra element information

```
<body>
<hr />
</body>
```

<pre>

The `<pre>` element contains preformatted text. Text in a pre element is displayed in a fixed-width font (usually Courier), and preserves both spaces and line breaks.

Syntax `<pre> ... </pre>`

Standard

Attribute	Value
class	classname
id	unique identifier
style	style definition
title	extra element information

```
<body>

<pre>
The quick
      brown fox
            jumped over

 the lazy dog.
</pre>

</body>
```

Block Level Elements Example

Here is a browser preview of the block level elements described in this section.

> The blockquote element is used to indicate the quotation of a large section of text from another source.Using the default HTML styling of most web browsers, it will indent the right and left margins both on the display and in printed form.

This is a <div> block level element.

Heading Level 1

Heading Level 2

Heading Level 3

Heading Level 4

Heading Level 5

Heading Level 6

The quick brown fox jumped over the lazy dog.

```
The quick
      brown fox
                jumped over
     the lazy dog.
```

The following is the HTML code which produced the previous browser example.

```
<!DOCTYPE HTML>

<html lang="en">

<head>

<title>Block Level Elements</title>

<link href="03_style.css" rel="stylesheet" type="text/css" media="screen">

</head>

<body>

<blockquote class="quote" id="definition1" style="border: 1px solid #E0DFE3;
padding: 3px;" cite="http://en.wikipedia.org/wiki/Blockquote_element">
The blockquote element is used to indicate the quotation of a large section
of text from another source.Using the default HTML styling of most web
browsers, it will indent the right and left margins both on the display
and in printed form.
</blockquote>

<div style="background-color:#CCCCCC; border: 1px dashed #0033FF; padding:
3px;">
This is a &lt;div&gt; block level element.
</div>

<h1>Heading Level 1</h1>
<h2>Heading Level 2</h2>
<h3>Heading Level 3</h3>
<h4>Heading Level 4</h4>
<h5>Heading Level 5</h5>
<h6>Heading Level 6</h6>

<hr />

<p>The quick brown fox jumped over the lazy dog.</p>

<pre>
The quick
      brown fox
            jumped over
     the lazy dog.
</pre>

</body>
```

List Elements

List elements reside within the `<body> ... </body>` of the HTML page and define specific block elements. In this section we will cover the following HTML elements:

- <dl>
  - <dt>
  - <dd>
- <ol> / <ul>
  - <li>

<dl>

The `<dl>` element defines the outer boundary of a definition list.

Syntax `<dl> ... </dl>`

Standard

Attribute	Value
class	classname
id	unique identifier
style	style definition
title	extra element information

```
<body>

<dl>
...
</dl>

</body>
```

<dt>

The `<dt>` element defines a term (an item) in a definition list.

Syntax `<dt> ... </dt>`

Standard

Attribute	Value
class	classname
id	unique identifier
style	style definition
title	extra element information

```
<body>

<dl>
   <dt>dog</dt>
   <dt>cat</dt>
</dl>

</body>
```

<dd>

The `<dd>` element defines a description of a term in a definition list.

Syntax `<dd> ... </dd>`

Standard

Attribute	Value
class	classname
id	unique identifier
style	style definition
title	extra element information

```
<body>

<dl>
   <dt>dog</dt>
   <dd> a domesticated canid, Canis familiaris, bred
in many varieties.</dd>
   <dt>cat</dt>
   <dd> a small domesticated carnivore, Felis
domestica or F. catus, bred in a number of
varieties.</dd>
</dl>

</body>
```

<ol> / <ul>

The `<ol>` element defines the outer boundary of an ordered list (numbered list).

The `<ul>` element defines the outer boundary of an unordered list (bulleted list).

Syntax
```
<ol> ... </ol>
<ol> ... </ol>
```

Standard

Attribute	Value
class	classname
id	unique identifier
style	style definition
title	extra element information

```
<body>

<ol>
...
</ol>

</body>
```

```
<body>

<ul>
...
</ul>

</body>
```

<li>

The `<li>` element defines a list item and is used in both ordered (`<ol>`) and unordered (`<ul>`) lists.

Syntax `<li> ... </li>`

Standard

Attribute	Value
class	classname
id	unique identifier
style	style definition
title	extra element information

```
<body>

<ol>
   <li>Fruit</li>
   <li>Vegetables</li>
</ol>

</body>
```

```
<body>

<ul>
   <li>Fruit</li>
   <li>Vegetables</li>
</ul>

</body>
```

Lists can be nested to create sub-levels for both ordered (<ol>) and unordered (<ul>) lists.

```
<body>

<ol>
   <li>Fruit</li>
   <ol>
      <li>Apple</li>
      <li>Banana</li>
      <li>Orange</li>
   </ol>
   <li>Vegetables</li>
   <ol>
      <li>Green Pepper</li>
      <li>Onion</li>
      <li>Tomato</li>
   </ol>
</ol>

</body>
```

```
<body>

<ul>
   <li>Fruit</li>
   <ul>
      <li>Apple</li>
      <li>Banana</li>
      <li>Orange</li>
   </ul>
   <li>Vegetables</li>
   <ul>
      <li>Green Pepper</li>
      <li>Onion</li>
      <li>Tomato</li>
   </ul>
</ul>

</body>
```

List Elements Example

Here is a browser preview of the list elements described in this section.

dog
: a domesticated canid, Canis familiaris, bred in many varieties.

cat
: a small domesticated carnivore, Felis domestica or F. catus, bred in a number of varieties.

1. Fruit
    1. Apple
    2. Banana
    3. Orange
2. Vegetables
    1. Green Pepper
    2. Onion
    3. Tomato

- Fruit
    - Apple
    - Banana
    - Orange
- Vegetables
    - Green Pepper
    - Onion
    - Tomato

The following is the HTML code which produced the previous browser example.

```
<!DOCTYPE HTML>

<html lang="en">

<head>

<title>List Elements</title>

<link href="03_style.css" rel="stylesheet" type="text/css" media="screen">

</head>

<body>

<dl>
    <dt>dog</dt>
    <dd> a domesticated canid, Canis familiaris,  bred in many varieties.</dd>
    <dt>cat</dt>
    <dd> a small domesticated carnivore, Felis domestica  or F. catus,
    bred in a number of varieties.</dd>
</dl>

<ol>
    <li>Fruit</li>
    <ol>
        <li>Apple</li>
        <li>Banana</li>
        <li>Orange</li>
    </ol>
    <li>Vegetables</li>
    <ol>
        <li>Green Pepper</li>
        <li>Onion</li>
        <li>Tomato</li>
    </ol>
</ol>

<ul>
    <li>Fruit</li>
    <ul>
        <li>Apple</li>
        <li>Banana</li>
        <li>Orange</li>
    </ul>
    <li>Vegetables</li>
    <ul>
        <li>Green Pepper</li>
        <li>Onion</li>
        <li>Tomato</li>
    </ul>
</ul>

</body>
```

Table Elements

Table elements reside within the `<body> ... </body>` of the HTML page and define specific block elements. In this section we will cover the following HTML elements:

- <table>
  - <caption>
  - <colgroup>
  - <thead>
  - <tfoot>
  - <tbody>
  - <tr>
    - <th>
    - <td>

<table>

The `<table>` element defines an HTML table.

Syntax `<table> ... </table>`

Optional

Attribute	Value
border width of the borders around a table	pixels
cellpadding space between the cell wall and the cell content	pixels
cellspacing space between cells	pixels
width width of a table	pixels %

Standard

Attribute	Value
class	classname
id	unique identifier
style	style definition
title	extra element information

```
<body>

<table border="1px" cellpadding="3px"
cellspacing="1px" width="100%">
...
</table>

</body>
```

<caption>

The `<caption>` element defines a caption for the HTML table.

Syntax `<caption> ... </caption>`

Standard

Attribute	Value
class	classname
id	unique identifier
style	style definition
title	extra element information

```
<body>

<table border="1px" cellpadding="3px"
cellspacing="1px" width="100%">
<caption>June 2012</caption>
...
</table>

</body>
```

<colgroup>

The `<colgroup>` element a group of columns in a table for formatting.

Syntax `<colgroup> ... </colgroup>`

Optional

Attribute	Value
align aligns the content in a column group	left right center justify
span the number of columns a colgroup should span	number
valign vertical alignment of the content in a column group	top middle bottom baseline
width the width of a column group	pixels % relative_length

Standard

Attribute	Value
class	classname
id	unique identifier
style	style definition
title	extra element information

```
<body>

<table border="1px" cellpadding="3px"
cellspacing="1px" width="100%">
<caption> June 2012</caption>
<colgroup span="5" width="14%"></colgroup>
<colgroup span="2" width="15%"></colgroup>
...
</table>

</body>
```

<thead>

The `<thead>` element defines the header content group in an HTML table.

Syntax `<thead> ... </thead>`

Optional

Attribute	Value
align aligns the content in a column group	left right center justify
valign vertical alignment of the content in a column group	top middle bottom baseline

Standard

Attribute	Value
class	classname
id	unique identifier
style	style definition
title	extra element information

```
<body>

<table border="1px" cellpadding="3px"
cellspacing="1px" width="100%">
<caption> June 2012</caption>
<colgroup span="5" width="14%"></colgroup>
<colgroup span="2" width="15%"></colgroup>
   <thead>
   ...
   </thead>
...
</table>

</body>
```

<tfoot>

The `<tfoot>` element defines the footer content group in an HTML table.

Syntax `<tfoot> ... </tfoot>`

Optional

Attribute	Value
align aligns the content in a column group	left right center justify
valign vertical alignment of the content in a column group	top middle bottom baseline

Standard

Attribute	Value
class	classname
id	unique identifier
style	style definition
title	extra element information

```
<body>

<table border="1px" cellpadding="3px"
cellspacing="1px" width="100%">
<caption> June 2012</caption>
<colgroup span="5" width="14%"></colgroup>
<colgroup span="2" width="15%"></colgroup>
   <thead>
   ...
   </thead>
   <tfoot>
   ...
   </tfoot>
...
</table>

</body>
```

<tbody>

The `<tbody>` element defines the body content group in an HTML table.

Syntax `<tbody> ... </tbody>`

Optional

Attribute	Value
align aligns the content in a column group	left right center justify
valign vertical alignment of the content in a column group	top middle bottom baseline

Standard

Attribute	Value
class	classname
id	unique identifier
style	style definition
title	extra element information

```
<body>

<table border="1px" cellpadding="3px"
cellspacing="1px" width="100%">
<caption> June 2012</caption>
<colgroup span="5" width="14%"></colgroup>
<colgroup span="2" width="15%"></colgroup>
   <thead>
   ...
   </thead>
   <tfoot>
   ...
   </tfoot>
   <tbody>
   ...
   </tbody>
</table>

</body>
```

<tr>

The `<tr>` element defines a row in an HTML table.

Syntax `<tr> ... </tr>`

Optional

Attribute	Value
align aligns the content in a column group	left right center justify
valign vertical alignment of the content in a column group	top middle bottom baseline

Standard

Attribute	Value
class	classname
id	unique identifier
style	style definition
title	extra element information

```
<body>

<table border="1px" cellpadding="3px"
cellspacing="1px" width="100%">
<caption> June 2012</caption>
<colgroup span="5" width="14%"></colgroup>
<colgroup span="2" width="15%"></colgroup>
   <thead>
      <tr>
      ...
      </tr>
   </thead>
   <tfoot>
      <tr>
      ...
      </tr>
   </tfoot>
   <tbody>
      <tr>
      ...
      </tr>
   </tbody>
</table>

</body>
```

<th>

The `<th>` element defines a header cell in an HTML table.

Syntax `<th> ... </th>`

Optional

Attribute	Value
align aligns the content in a column group	left right center justify
colspan number of columns a cell should span	number
valign vertical alignment of the content in a column group	top middle bottom baseline

Standard

Attribute	Value
class	classname
id	unique identifier
style	style definition
title	extra element information

```
<body>

<table border="1px" cellpadding="3px"
cellspacing="1px" width="100%">
<caption> June 2012</caption>
<colgroup span="5" width="14%"></colgroup>
<colgroup span="2" width="15%"></colgroup>
   <thead>
      <tr>
         <th>Sat</th>
         <th>Sun</th>
         <th>Mon</th>
         <th>Tue</th>
         <th>Wed</th>
         <th>Thu</th>
         <th>Fri</th>
      </tr>
   </thead>
   <tfoot>
      <tr>
      ...
      </tr>
   </tfoot>
   <tbody>
      <tr>
      ...
      </tr>
   </tbody>
</table>

</body>
```

<td>

The `<td>` element defines a data cell in an HTML table.

Syntax `<td> ... </td>`

Optional

Attribute	Value
align aligns the content in a column group	left right center justify
colspan number of columns a cell should span	number
valign vertical alignment of the content in a column group	top middle bottom baseline

Standard

Attribute	Value
class	classname
id	unique identifier
style	style definition
title	extra element information

```
<body>

<table border="1px" cellpadding="3px"
cellspacing="1px" width="100%">
<caption> June 2012</caption>
<colgroup span="5" width="14%"></colgroup>
<colgroup span="2" width="15%"></colgroup>
   <thead>
      <tr>
         <th>Sat</th>
         <th>Sun</th>
         <th>Mon</th>
         <th>Tue</th>
         <th>Wed</th>
         <th>Thu</th>
         <th>Fri</th>
      </tr>
   </thead>
   <tfoot>
      <tr>
         <td colspan="7">What A Week!</td>
      </tr>
   </tfoot>
   <tbody>
      <tr>
         <td>16</td>
         <td>17</td>
         <td>18</td>
         <td>19</td>
         <td>20</td>
         <td>21</td>
         <td>22</td>
      </tr>
   </tbody>
</table>

</body>
```

Table Elements Example

Here is a browser preview of the table elements described in this section.

June 2012

Sat	Sun	Mon	Tue	Wed	Thu	Fri
16	17	18	19	20	21	22
What A Week!						

The following is the HTML code which produced the previous browser example.

```
<!DOCTYPE HTML>

<html lang="en">

<head>

<title>Table Elements</title>

<link href="03_style.css" rel="stylesheet" type="text/css" media="screen">

</head>

<body>

<table border="1px" cellpadding="3px" cellspacing="1px" width="100%">
<caption>June 2012</caption>
<colgroup span="2" width="10%"></colgroup>
<colgroup span="5" width="16%"></colgroup>
    <thead>
        <tr>
            <th>Sat</th>
            <th>Sun</th>
            <th>Mon</th>
            <th>Tue</th>
            <th>Wed</th>
            <th>Thu</th>
            <th>Fri</th>
        </tr>
    </thead>
    <tfoot>
        <tr>
            <td colspan="7">What A Week!</td>
        </tr>
    </tfoot>
    <tbody>
        <tr>
            <td>16</td>
            <td>17</td>
            <td>18</td>
            <td>19</td>
            <td>20</td>
            <td>21</td>
            <td>22</td>
        </tr>
    </tbody>
</table>

</body>
```

Form Elements

Form elements reside within the `<body> ... </body>` of the HTML page and define specific block elements. In this section we will cover the following HTML elements:

- <form>
  - <fieldset>
    - <legend>
  - <input />
    - <label>
  - <textarea>
  - <select>
    - <optgroup>
    - <option>
  - <button>

<form>

The `<form>` element defines an HTML form for user input.

Syntax `<form> ... </form>`

Required

Attribute	Value
action where to send the form-data when a form is submitted	URL

Optional

Attribute	Value
method how to send form-data	get post
name unique the name for a form	name
target	_blank _self _parent _top

Standard

Attribute	Value
class	classname
id	unique identifier
style	style definition
title	extra element information

```
<body>

<form>
...
<form>

</body>
```

<fieldset>

The `<fieldset>` element defines a border around elements in an HTML form.

Syntax `<fieldset> ... </fieldset>`

Standard

Attribute	Value
class	classname
id	unique identifier
style	style definition
title	extra element information

```
<body>

<form>
   <fieldset>
   ...
   </fieldset>
<form>

</body>
```

<legend>

The `<fieldset>` element defines a caption for a fieldset element.

Syntax `<fieldset> ... </fieldset>`

Standard

Attribute	Value
accesskey keyboard shortcut to access an element	character
class	classname
id	unique identifier
style	style definition
title	extra element information

```
<body>

<form>
   <fieldset>
      <legend>Personal Information</legend>
      ...
   </fieldset>
<form>

</body>
```

<input />

The `<input>` element defines an input control in an HTML form.

Syntax `<input> ... </input>`

Optional

Attribute	Value
alt alternate text for an image input	text (type="image" only)
checked element should be preselected when the page loads	checked (type="checkbox" or type="radio" only)
maxlength maximum length of an input field	number
name	name
readonly	readonly
size width of an input field	number
src URL to an image to display as a submit button	URL (only for type="image")

type type of input element	button checkbox file hidden image password radio reset submit text
value	value

Standard

Attribute	Value
class	classname
id	unique identifier
style	style definition
tabindex	number
title	extra element information

```
<body>
<form>
   <fieldset>
      <legend>Personal Information</legend>
      First Name: <input type="text" name="fname" />
      <br />
      Last Name: <input type="text" name="lname" />
   </fieldset>
<form>
</body>
```

<label>

The `<label>` element defines an input element label.

Syntax `<label> ... </label>`

Optional

Attribute	Value
for which form element a label is bound to	element

Standard

Attribute	Value
accesskey	character
class	classname
id	unique identifier
style	style definition
title	extra element information

```
<body>

<form>
   <input type="radio" name="sex" id="male" />
   <label for="male">Male</label>
   <br />
   <input type="radio" name="sex" id="female" />
   <label for="female">Female</label>
<form>

</body>
```

<textarea>

The `<textarea>` element defines multi-line text input element.

Syntax `<textarea> ... </textarea>`

Required

Attribute	Value
cols width of a text-area	number
rows number of rows	number

Optional

Attribute	Value
disabled field should be disabled	disabled
name	name_of_textarea
readonly field should be read only	readonly

Standard

Attribute	Value
accesskey	character
class	classname
id	unique identifier
style	style definition
tabindex	number
title	extra element information

```
<body>

<form>
   <textarea cols="10" rows="2">The quick brown fox
jumped over the lazzy dog.</textarea>
<form>

</body>
```

<select>

The `<select>` element is used to create a select list.

Syntax `<select> ... </select>`

Optional

Attribute	Value
disabled field should be disabled	disabled
multiple user can select multiple options	multiple
name	name_of_textarea
size number of visible options	number

Standard	Attribute	Value
	accesskey	character
	class	classname
	id	unique identifier
	style	style definition
	tabindex tab order of an element	number
	title	extra element information

```
<body>

<form>
   <select>
   ...
   </select>
<form>

</body>
```

<optgroup>

The `<optgroup>` element defines group of related options in a select list.

Syntax `<optgroup> ... </optgroup>`

Required

Attribute	Value
label	text

Optional

Attribute	Value
disabled field should be disabled	disabled

Standard

Attribute	Value
class	classname
id	unique identifier
style	style definition
title	extra element information

```
<body>

<form>
   <select>
      <optgroup label="Fruit">
      ...
      </optgroup>
   </select>
<form>

</body>
```

<option>

The `<option>` element defines an option in a select list.

Syntax `<option> ... </option>`

Optional

Attribute	Value
disabled field should be disabled	disabled
label	text
selected option should be selected by default	selected
value the value to be sent to a server when a form is submitted	text

Standard

Attribute	Value
class	classname
id	unique identifier
style	style definition
title	extra element information

```
<body>

<form>
   <select>
      <optgroup label="Fruit">
         <option>Apple</option>
         <option>Banana</option>
         <option>Orange</option>
      </optgroup>
   </select>
<form>

</body>
```

<button>

The `<button>` element defines an option in a select list.

Syntax `<button> ... </button>`

Optional

Attribute	Value
disabled field should be disabled	disabled
name	name
type option should be selected by default	button reset submit
value the value to be sent to a server when a form is submitted	text

Standard

Attribute	Value
accesskey	character
class	classname
id	unique identifier
style	style definition
tabindex tab order of an element	number
title	extra element information

```
<body>

<form>
   <button type="button">Click Me!</button>
<form>

</body>
```

Form Elements Example

Here is a browser preview of the form elements described in this section.

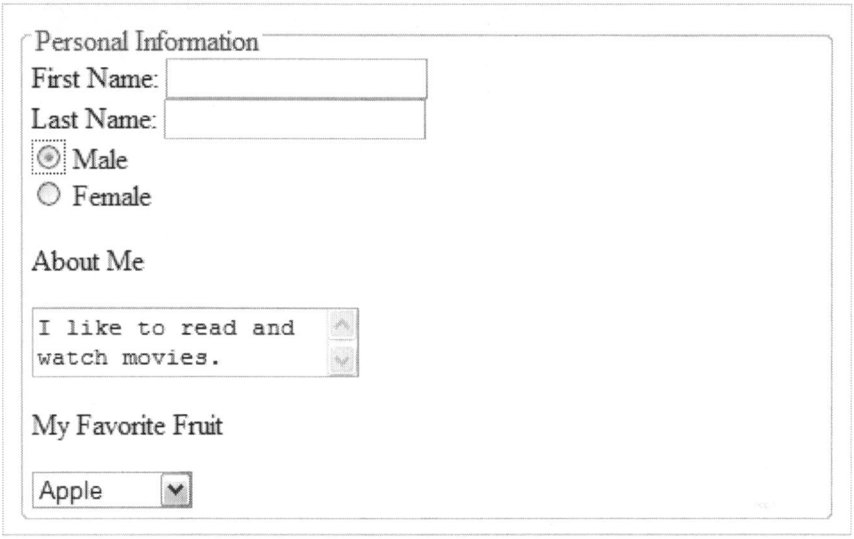

The following is the HTML code which produced the previous browser example.

```
<!DOCTYPE HTML>

<html lang="en">

<head>

<title>Form Elements</title>

<link href="03_style.css" rel="stylesheet" type="text/css" media="screen">

</head>

<body>

<form>
    <fieldset>
        <legend>Personal Information</legend>
        First Name: <input type="text" name="fname" /><br />
        Last Name: <input type="text" name="lname" /><br />
        <input type="radio" name="sex" id="male" />
        <label for="male">Male</label><br />
        <input type="radio" name="sex" id="female" />
        <label for="female">Female</label>
        <p>About Me</p>
        <textarea cols="20" rows="2">I like to read and watch
movies.</textarea>
        <p>My Favorite Fruit</p>
        <select>
            <optgroup label="Fruit">
                <option>Apple</option>
                <option>Banana</option>
                <option>Orange</option>
            </optgroup>
        </select>
    </fieldset>
</form>

</body>
```

Inline Elements

Inline elements reside within the `<body> ... </body>` of the HTML page. In this section we will cover the following HTML elements:

- <a>
- <abbr>
- <acronym>
-
- <iframe>
- <img />
- <span>
- <sub>
- <sup>

<a>

The `<a>` element defines an anchor for a hypertext link.

Syntax `<a> ... </a>`

Optional

Attribute	Value
href the destination of a link	URL
target where to open the linked document	_blank _parent _self _top

Standard

Attribute	Value
accesskey	character
class	classname
id	unique identifier
style	style definition
title	extra element information

```
<body>

<a href="http://www.google.com" target="_blank">

</body>
```

<abbr>

The `<abbr>` element defines an abbreviation.

Syntax `<abbr> ... </abbr>`

Standard

Attribute	Value
class	classname
id	unique identifier
style	style definition
title	extra element information

```
<body>

<p>The <abbr title="Hyper Text Markup
Language">HTML</abbr> is the basic language of the
web.</p>

</body>
```

<acronym>

The `<acronym>` element defines an acronym.

Syntax `<acronym> ... </acronym>`

Standard

Attribute	Value
class	classname
id	unique identifier
style	style definition
title	extra element information

```
<body>

<p>The <acronym title="Hyper Text Markup
Language">HTML</acronym> is the basic language of the
web.</p>

</body>
```


The `<br />` element defines a single line break.

Syntax `<br />`

Standard

Attribute	Value
class	classname
id	unique identifier
style	style definition
title	extra element information

```
<body>

<p>The quick brown fox jumped over the lazy dog.<br />
Then he jumped over the dog again.</p>

</body>
```

<iframe>

The `<iframe>` element defines an inline frame that contains another document.

Syntax `<iframe> ... </iframe>`

Optional

Attribute	Value
href the destination of a link	URL
target where to open the linked document	_blank _parent _self _top

Standard

Attribute	Value
class	classname
id	unique identifier
style	style definition
title	extra element information

```
<body>

<iframe src="http://www.google.com" width="100%"
height="300px">
   <p>Your browser does not support iframes.</p>
</iframe>

</body>
```

<img />

The `<img />` element defines an image.

Syntax `<img />`

Required

Attribute	Value
alt alternate text describing an image	text
src location of the image	URL

Optional

Attribute	Value
height	pixels %
longdesc URL to a document that contains a long description of an image	URL
width	pixels %

Standard

Attribute	Value
class	classname
id	unique identifier
style	style definition
title	extra element information

```
<body>

<img src=" http://www.cewebservices.com/logo_cews.png">

</body>
```

<span>

The `<span>` element defines an inline container.

Syntax `<span> ... </span>`

Standard

Attribute	Value
class	classname
id	unique identifier
style	style definition
title	extra element information

```
<body>

<p>The quick brown fox <span style="text-weight:
bold;">jumped</span> over the lazy dog.</p>

</body>
```

<sub>

The `<sub>` element defines subscripted text.

Syntax `<sub> ... </sub>`

Standard

Attribute	Value
class	classname
id	unique identifier
style	style definition
title	extra element information

```
<body>

<p>The quick brown fox <sub>jumped</sub> over the lazy
dog.</p>

</body>
```

<sup>

The `<sup>` element defines superscript text.

Syntax `<sup> ... </sup>`

Standard

Attribute	Value
class	classname
id	unique identifier
style	style definition
title	extra element information

```
<body>

<p>The quick brown fox <sup>jumped</sup> over the lazy
dog.</p>

</body>
```

Inline Elements Example

Here is a browser preview of the inline elements described in this section.

CE Web Services

HTML is the basic language of the web.

HTML is the basic language of the web.

The quick brown fox jumped over the lazy dog.
Then he jumped over the dog again.

CE Web Services

The quick brown fox jumped over the lazy dog.

The quick brown fox $_{\text{jumped}}$ over the lazy dog.

The quick brown fox ^{jumped} over the lazy dog.

The following is the HTML code which produced the previous browser example.

```
<!DOCTYPE HTML>

<html lang="en">

<head>

<title>Inline Elements</title>

<link href="03_style.css" rel="stylesheet" type="text/css" media="screen">

</head>

<body>

<a href="http://www.cewebservices.com" target="_blank">CE Web Services</a>

<p><abbr title="Hyper Text Markup Language">HTML</abbr> is
the basic language of the web.</p>

<p><acronym title="Hyper Text Markup Language">HTML</acronym> is
the basic language of the web.</p>

<p><br></p>

<p>The quick brown fox jumped over the lazy dog.<br />
Then he jumped over the dog again.</p>

<iframe src="http://www.cewebservices.com/studio/" width="100%" height="300px">
    <p>Your browser does not support iframes.</p>
</iframe>

<p>
<img src=" http://www.cewebservices.com/logo_cews.png">
</p>

<p>The quick brown fox <span style="text-weight: bold;">jumped</span>
over the lazy dog.</p>

<p>The quick brown fox <sub>jumped</sub> over the lazy dog.</p>

<p>The quick brown fox <sup>jumped</sup> over the lazy dog.</p>

</body>
```

Chapter 3

Conclusion

Conclusion

I sincerely hope you find this HTML reference useful. It contains most of the HTML elements I use every day. This has been a fun little project for me and maybe someday my sons will discover the same fulfilling enjoyment of creative problem solving that I have taken pleasure in over the years.

Reference Information

World Wide Web Consortium (W3C)
http://www.w3.org

W3Schools Online Web Tutorials
http://www.w3schools.com

HTML Help by The Web Design Group
http://www.htmlhelp.com

HTML Goodies: The Ultimate HTML Resource
http://www.htmlgoodies.com

Index

16661973R00065

Printed in Great Britain
by Amazon